Alfred Gurney

Our Catholic Inheritance in the Larger Hope

An Essay

Alfred Gurney

Our Catholic Inheritance in the Larger Hope
An Essay

ISBN/EAN: 9783337331337

Printed in Europe, USA, Canada, Australia, Japan

Cover: Foto ©Lupo / pixelio.de

More available books at **www.hansebooks.com**

OUR CATHOLIC INHERITANCE IN THE LARGER HOPE

AN ESSAY

BY

ALFRED GURNEY, M.A.

VICAR OF S. BARNABAS', PIMLICO

AUTHOR OF 'THE VISION OF THE EUCHARIST' 'A CHRISTMAS FAGGOT' ETC.

TOGETHER WITH A HISTORICAL APPENDIX

BY H. H. JEAFFRESON, M.A.

'At last I heard a voice upon the slope
Cry to the summit, "Is there any hope?"
To which an answer pealed from that high land,
But in a tongue no man could understand :
And on the glimmering limit far withdrawn,
God made Himself an awful rose of dawn'—TENNYSON

'Heaviness may endure for a night, but joy cometh in the morning'

'He shall see of the travail of His soul and shall be satisfied'

LONDON

KEGAN PAUL, TRENCH, & CO., 1 PATERNOSTER SQUARE

1888

Christ's question through the ages rings
   Unanswered by His Lips ; His Eyes
   Hold in their light of love replies
To all our silent questionings.

Ah ! silence is a sepulchre
   Where faded lips wax eloquent ;
   The question asked was surely meant
To make each soul a questioner.

Those silent Wounds, so dear and dread,
   Are all the answer that we need ;
   He is the Father's Word indeed,
So all things are interpreted.

Of old dwelt faith upon the earth ;
   Men walked with God, in daily toil
   Conversed with Him : who dares despoil
Mankind of rights that come from birth ?

' What rights ? ' the scoffer asks ; I say,
   ' Birthrights ; ' my Father's child, with Him
   I live my life ; my light is dim,
But hope anticipates the day

When, in the light of love revealed,
   All questions shall be answered, then
   Shall God be justified of men.
Alas ! for those who will not yield ;

Whom love repels, whose caitiff hearts
Will no home-courtesies fulfil,
Rebellious to a Father's Will,
Rejecting what His Hand imparts.

Must then the children's ranks be thinned?
God grant that on a coming day
These too might tread the homeward way,
Confessing ' Father, we have sinned.'

Then would He fold them to His Breast,
Aweary of their wandering,
And blithely would the angels sing—
ˣ The lost are found, and all are blest.'

From Manger, Cross, and Sepulchre,
Christ's question through the ages rings ;
His children of all questionings
Discern in Him the Answerer.

CAMPO SANTO, PISA, 1878.

———

The dead praise not Thee, O God, neither all they that
go down into hell.   The living, the living, he shall praise
Thee.

O Lord, deliver my soul ; the Lord is righteous, yea,
our God is merciful.   Deliver my soul from death, mine
eyes from tears, and my feet from falling, that I may sing a
new song unto Thee, and offer to Thee the sacrifice of
Thanksgiving.

The Lord is my Strength, and my Song, and is become
my Salvation.

The Right Hand of the Lord hath the pre-eminence, the
Right Hand of the Lord bringeth mighty things to pass.

I shall not die but live, and declare the works of the Lord.

The Lord hath chastened and corrected me, but He hath not given me over unto death.

Thou hast broken my bonds in sunder ; death is swallowed up in victory.

My soul is escaped as a bird out of the snare of the fowler.   The snare is broken, and I am delivered.

I will give thanks unto the Lord, for He is gracious, because His mercy endureth for ever.   Amen, Amen.

Paradise of the Christian Soul : ' Prayer for deliverance from everlasting death.'

PREFACE.

THE following paper was read before a Society of Priests, gathered together for conference, at St. Paul's Chapter House, on May 15, 1888. At the request of some of those who heard it, and whose wishes I could not disregard, I have consented to publish it.

In any matter of controversy it is a consolation to reflect that the Truth, which we are seeking to discern and embrace, must be, since it is God's Truth, infinitely grander and lovelier than any conception of it which our minds are able to entertain. By Him Who is the Living Truth we are apprehended ; may He, by the illuminating unction of His Blessed Spirit, enable us more perfectly to apprehend. So shall we learn 'to abound in Hope by the power of the Holy Ghost.'

Whitsuntide : 1888,

OUR CATHOLIC INHERITANCE IN THE LARGER HOPE.

—◦◦—

IN approaching so difficult a subject, I am glad to be free of the responsibility of having introduced it. The task before me is not to maintain any precarious doctrine, much less insist upon any conclusion, touching a matter which the Church has left open ; but merely to renew a discussion which was commenced with conspicuous ability at our last meeting. In attempting to uphold what I conceive to be the Scriptural doctrine of ' the Restitution of all things,' I am not joining issue with those who maintain everlasting punishment, for restitution must refer to deliverance not from the punishment of sin, but from sin itself.[1] It is surely quite conceivable that everlasting punishment may be the very means of deliverance. It is not the penal consequences of sin that the sinner, when brought to penitence, desires to escape from, but the

[1] Acts iii. 21.

pollution. For the true penitent knows that judgment is salvation; for him punishment is transfigured into penance, and to such a one penance is ever welcome. The penitent robber did not ask or wish to be taken down from his cross; he endured it, and died on it, well content to be remembered by his Absolver and his King.

But if we look more fully and carefully into the matter, we shall, I think, come to the conclusion that sin is its own punishment,[1] and in that case the punishment of necessity ceases when sin is abolished. When that blessed result is arrived at, the bitterness of any pains and penalties that may still remain will be immediately and effectually sweetened, for the sufferer will gladly acquiesce in them, and indeed will be ready to enforce them against himself.

The question before us therefore is, not will punishment endure for ever, but will sin? To that question the Scriptures, as interpreted by the Church, seem to me to give a negative answer. Are we not told that Christ was manifested to destroy the works of the devil? that He is the Saviour of all men? and that it is the Father's good pleasure to sum up all things in Him, and reconcile them to Himself?

To assert the permanence of evil looks to me

---

[1] 'L'enfer c'est le péché même, l'enfer c'est d'être éloigné de Dieu.' —Bossuet.

very much like a denial of the victory of Christ ; and
when it is the evil of never-ending rebellion against
God, rejection of His Love, and defiance of His
Authority, on the part of children whom He has
created and redeemed, it is a doctrine which certainly
seems to contradict not only many plain statements
of Holy Scripture, but the whole tenor of the Gospel
message as delivered and apprehended by the Church.
It is not, of course, denied that a belief in everlasting punishment has been for centuries the prevalent
belief among Catholics both within and outside the
Roman obedience ; but it should be remembered
that such a doctrine has no place in any one of the
Catholic Symbols, and has been rejected by doctors
of the greatest authority ; so that it has never ob-
tained the footing and currency in Catholic schools
of thought which belong to it in the Protestant
sects.[1]

Moreover, the real matter for consideration, as has

[1] ‘What is called orthodox Protestantism has clung with a singular
tenacity to the doctrine of eternal punishment, which forms, if I am
not mistaken, one of nine articles of faith, constituting the bond of union
of the Evangelical Alliance’ (Oxenham, *Catholic Eschatology*, p. xxv).
It is the doctrine of Lutherans, of Calvinists, and of Presbyterians, as
shown by their authoritative documents, the 17th Article of the Confession of Augsburg, the 15th Canon of the Synod of Dort, and the
Westminster Confession of Faith. The latter declares that ‘By the
decree of God, for His honour and glory, some men and angels are
predestined unto everlasting life, and others foreordained to everlasting
death’ (Ch. iii. Art. 6).

been already indicated, is the permanence of sin, not of punishment; and the distinction is one with which the Church's penitential system has made her children familiar. 'The penalty of original sin is,' according to the decision of Innocent III., 'the deprivation of the vision of God'; but that can hardly be regarded as a punishment which consists in the withholding from any of a benefit for the enjoyment of which they have no capacity. The following words concerning the condition of such souls are taken from an article in the 'Dublin Review': 'The majority of theologians, with S. Thomas and Scotus at their head, maintain that those lost ones, though knowing full well that there is an unspeakable happiness which they are never to enjoy, yet feel no sadness or pain of any kind from the knowledge of this privation—God's omnipotent Hand so cradling their minds in this calm repose. Yet farther still : Suarez and others, still following the same angelic doctor, hold that they enjoy a permanent and undisturbed natural beatitude of the understanding and the will; knowing God as perfectly as He can be known through His creatures, and for all eternity loving Him and enjoying Him as thus known.' [1]

Dr. Pusey has reminded us that 'the Church has her long list of Saints; she has not inserted one

---

[1] *Dublin Review*, January 1873.

name in any catalogue of the damned.' No, she has
not, and she could not; not even the name of the
apostle who betrayed his Lord. Motherlike she
prays for all men, and she could not pray for all if
she did not entertain an invincible hope for all,
for every Christian prayer is of necessity an act of
hope ; there is no such thing as despairing prayer.
Both Dr. Arnold and Mr. Jukes have dwelt strongly
on the service rendered to truth and charity by the
observance of All Souls' Day, a festival the full significance of which is thus admirably expounded by the
latter : ' The fact that the Church for many hundred
years has had an All Souls' Day as well as an All
Saints' Day in her Calendar is itself a witness that
she may have been teaching far more than some of
her sons as yet have learnt from her. For why did
the Church ordain a celebration for All Souls as well
as for All Saints, but because, spite of her children's
contradiction, she believed that, like her Lord, she is
truly linked to all, and with Him is ordained at last
to gather all. And why does All Souls' Day follow
All Saints', but to declare that All Saints should
reach All Souls, going before them indeed, yet going
before them to be a blessing to them. For indeed
All Saints are to All Souls as the first-born to their
younger brethren, elect to be both kings and priests
to them ; or as the firstfruits to the harvest, the

pledge of what is to come, if not also the means to bring it about in due season.' [1]

Within the precincts of the Church, moreover, the whole outlook into the future has been brightened and illuminated by the assurance that there is a time and place for purification and deepening penitence on the other side of death. The words of S. Peter, read at all the altars of the Church of England on Easter Eve, would seem to make this certain : Christ, Who suffered for sins, the Just for the unjust, that He might bring us to God, 'went and preached to the spirits in prison, which sometime were disobedient.' [2]

The Flood, S. Peter tells us, was a Baptism ; it drowned the world, it floated the ark. Noah and his family were saved, not only from the waters, but by the waters in which others perished. But those sinners, the inhabitants of a lost world, and so representative of all sinners, were, the Apostle intimates, delivered from the doom of an endless perdition by the victory of Christ. His preaching in Hades liberated ' the prisoners of hope.' In two passages of the ' Stromata ' S. Clement of Alexandria speaks of the Apostles as being after death 'imitators of their Master,' and participating in this blessed ministry of emancipation. [3] The belief in the purification wrought by a baptism of fire after death, justified by many passages

---

[1] *Restitution*, p. 45.   [2] I Peter iii. 19, 20.   [3] ii. 9 ; vi. 6.

of Holy Writ, has from the first commended itself to the Christian conscience and understanding, and has found expression in the universal practice of prayers for the dead—a practice sanctioned by instinct, by reason, by Scripture, and by the uniform tradition of the Church. 'One witness, at least, to the truth of wider happier thoughts as to the state of the dead than have recently prevailed among us, was borne with no faltering voice, in no indistinct accents, by the Church of the first ages. In every form, from the solemn Liturgies, which embodied the belief of the profoundest thinkers and truest worshippers, to the simple words of hope and love which were traced over the graves of the poor, her voice went up, without a doubt or misgiving, in prayers for the souls of the departed ;'—these are the beautiful words with which Dean Plumptre introduces the conclusion of his grand sermon, which he has since expanded into a book,[1] on 'The Spirits in Prison.'[2]

In order fully to elucidate the subject under consideration, a threefold effort seems to me to be required : (1) it is necessary to obtain the judgment of competent scholars as to the exact meaning of certain Greek words which constantly recur in this contro-

[1] P. 25.
[2] See *Ancient Prayers for the Departed*, quoted by Dr. Pusey; *Everlasting Punishment*, pp. 121-124 ; and chapters v.-ix. in Canon Luckock's admirable book *After Death*.

versy; (2) to consider the meaning of the various passages, not separated from their context, which are relied on by those who maintain that the permanence of sin is part of the divine revelation, comparing them with numerous other passages that appear to contradict them and to point to an opposite conclusion; and (3) to look at the Bible itself in its context, as the written tradition and statute law of the Church, not to be interpreted without reference to her common law and unwritten tradition, and the whole body of her gathered and treasured spiritual wisdom.

(1) In most of the modern books dealing with Eschatology with which I am acquainted, the words to which I refer are enumerated and discussed, and the discussion is one with which we must all be more or less familiar. It will not, I think, be asserted by anyone who has carefully considered the passages where the word occurs, that *αἰώνιος* is the same as 'everlasting,' or that *κόλασις* signifies retributive and not remedial and corrective 'punishment,' or that *κρίσις* is accurately translated 'damnation.' There are three Greek words for which the English word 'hell' stands in our Bibles as an equivalent, and in each case to the word so used its ordinarily accepted meaning must be denied, if it is in any way to represent the Greek. For 'Tartarus,' 'Hades,' and 'Gehenna' do not even suggest the idea of endless torments. When all these

mistranslations, and not a few others that might be named, are corrected, the texts usually quoted in support of the popular teaching about the destiny of lost souls begin to assume a very different complexion. Into these questions of verbal criticism, however, I do not propose to enter now. All who have studied the question are familiar with them, and it can hardly, I think, be seriously maintained that there is among scholars any important disagreement or perplexity as to the meaning of the terms employed.

(2) If we turn then from the investigation of words to that of passages, chapters, books of the Bible, the conviction grows and deepens (if I may judge of the experience of others by my own) that our largest, loftiest hopes do not go beyond that which Scripture warrants, and are justified by page after page of the inspired volume. Canon Farrar's hastily written book is, in my judgment, weakened and disfigured by the passionate declamation with which it abounds, and which is specially to be deplored in the treatment of a subject that demands above all things sobriety and reserve ; but I find in it a statement which my whole heart gladly endorses. Speaking of the witness of the Bible, he says, 'To adduce all the passages which deepen in my mind the trust in Eternal Hope would be to transcribe one half of the Scriptures ; rarely do I read the daily Psalms or the daily Lessons without

meeting with expressions which seem to run directly counter to the common doctrine.' [1]

I must rest content with the examination of a very few out of very many passages, and I will take those which are most frequently and most confidently appealed to by those who reject the doctrine of Restitution. It is a true observation of Charles Kingsley's that the parable of Dives and Lazarus is 'the one instance in which our Lord professedly opens the secrets of the next world;' and he goes on to point out that 'He there represents Dives as still Abraham's child, under no despair, not cut off from Abraham's sympathy, and under a direct moral training, of which you see the fruit. He is gradually weaned from the selfish desire of indulgence for himself to love and care for his brethren, a divine step forward in his life which of itself proves him not to be lost. The impossibility of Lazarus getting to him, or *vice versâ*, expresses plainly the great truth that, each being where he ought to be at that time, interchange of place (*i.e.* of spiritual state) is impossible. But it says nothing against Dives rising out of his torment, when he has learnt the lesson of it, and going where he ought to go.' [2] As a friend of mine once shrewdly observed : 'Dives must learn to make his appeal, not to "Father Abraham," but to Abraham's Father,

[1] *Eternal Hope*, p. 217.   [2] *Life*, p. 153.

and then the gulf of separation will be quickly crossed.'

There are perhaps no words in the whole Bible which, on examination, more powerfully encourage and sustain the hope of the ultimate restoration of all men than those which relate to fire. All through the sacred story of God's dealings with man, in both Testaments, we find it used by Him for the accomplishment of His gracious purposes. There was the burning bush, with its great revelation of the Name of God, and its foreshadowing of the Incarnation ; there was the pillar, a cloud by day, a fire by night, which guided and sheltered the Pilgrim-Church in the wilderness ; it was in fire that God revealed Himself on Mount Sinai ; fire fell from heaven upon the altar of burnt sacrifice to burn everlastingly, for it was distinctly ordained 'it shall not be quenched ';[1] the touch of fire liberated the sweet odours of the frank-incense at the golden altar of incense in the Holy Place ; fire, enkindled by the angel's staff, rose up out of the rock and consumed the sacrifice of Gideon ; God declared Himself at Carmel, on the occasion of Elijah's sacrifice, to be a God Who answers prayer by fire ; with a fiery chariot and horses of fire the prophet went up to heaven ; a live coal from the altar of sacrifice purged the lips of Isaiah ; 'a fire infolding

---

[1] Lev. vi. 13 ; πῦρ οὐ σβεσθήσεται.

itself' was the first thing that met the eyes of Ezekiel
as the heavenly vision opened to him ; not only from
fire, but by fire, were the three Hebrew children
saved, and instrumental in saving their nation, and
in the midst of the flames the Son of God was revealed ; the Same Who is represented by Malachi as
purifying the sons of Levi with refiner's fire. 'The
breath of the Lord' is that stream of brimstone which
kindles Tophet,[1] and only those who walk righteously
with God can 'dwell with the devouring Fire,' 'with
everlasting burnings.'[2]

And in the New Testament no less wonderful
are the revelations and deliverances wrought by fire.
The Baptist proclaims himself the herald and fore-
runner of Another Who shall baptise with the Holy
Ghost and with fire, and by Whom the chaff shall be
burnt up with fire unquenchable ; no sooner is Christ
exalted to the Throne of His Glory than the Promise
is fulfilled, and the Holy Ghost, 'the Spirit of judgment and of burning,' is revealed by the Pentecostal
tongues of fire ;[3] His own baptism of fire was on the
Mount of Transfiguration ; S. Paul, speaking of the
fire of God as that which is to test every man's work,
declares that even he, whose works fail to stand that
test and are destroyed, is nevertheless himself saved

---

[1] Isaiah xxx. 33.   [2] Isaiah xxxiii. 14, 15.
[3] Isaiah iv. 4.

by fire ;[1] the writer of the Epistle to the Hebrews represents the ministers of God to be 'a flame of fire ' ;[2] S. Peter speaks of the heavens being on fire and dissolved as preparatory to the incoming of victorious righteousness for the inhabitation of new heavens and a new earth ;[3] the beloved Disciple beheld, when the door of heaven opened to his anointed eyes, seven lamps of fire burning before the Throne of God ; and, as though interpreting the whole series, the Divine Master solemnly declares, ' I am come to send fire on the earth ' ; and ' Every one shall be salted with fire ' ;[4] it must be so, if a man is to become like his Father in heaven, and be made a partaker of the Divine Nature, ' for our God is a consuming Fire.'[5]

The Bible is full, no doubt, of passages recording destructions wrought by fire ; but they do but illustrate the familiar doctrine, of which the Christian Font is the abiding symbol, that death is the gate of life, that the seed is not quickened except it die. Sodom is a notable instance ; for the destruction of Sodom by fire was a divine chastisement which punished the abounding wickedness of a profligate city, and St. Jude[6] speaks of it in a manner that at first

[1] 1 Cor. iii. 15.   [2] Heb. i. 7.
[3] 2 Peter iii. 12, 13.   [4] Luke xii. 49 ; Mark ix. 49.
[5] Heb. xii. 29.   [6] St. Jude, 7.

sight might lead us to suppose that here at all events was a punishment that left no hope of recovery. But we turn to Ezekiel xvi., and there we find that Sodom is restored no less than Jerusalem and Samaria.[1]

Looked at in the light of these passages, and many more that might be quoted, I cannot but feel that the concluding words of the Athanasian Psalm, so faithfully echoing the words of our Lord's own parable of Judgment, are invested with the true awfulness that belongs to them, the awfulness which is inseparable from Divine Compassion: ' There is Mercy with Thee, therefore shalt Thou be feared.'[2] It is surely Mercy, exercised towards us by One Whom we have wronged, that constrains manly fear. Such fear is the beginning of spiritual wisdom ; it issues in generous penitence ; and so the wrong is righted.

There is one passage which perhaps more than any other has been relied on and appealed to by the deniers of universal Restitution—the passage in which our Lord rebukes the blasphemy against the Holy Ghost. Certainly there are no more awful words in Holy Scripture ; but it seems to me that, when so applied, they are altogether misunderstood. One thing they appear to imply, that for certain sins there is forgiveness in the next world, the sin against the Holy Ghost not being one of these. Of that sin

---

[1] Verses 53, 55.   [2] Psalm cxxx. 4.

our Lord says that for it there is no forgiveness 'either in this age or the coming age,' for so surely, having regard to God's revealed purpose with reference to 'the ages,' it should be translated.[1] It may be that all other sins vanish, together with the ignorance that caused them, when the soul awakes with vision cleared and enlightened after the sleep of death; but that that blindness of the soul to God the Holy Ghost, that obstinate rejection of Him, towards which all sin tends, but to which it perhaps seldom attains, requires a severer discipline to correct it, a longer and more piercing purgation to clear it away. The sin of ignorance is put away by the sinner as soon as ignorance itself is taken away; the sin of wilful rejection needs nothing less than that bruising with a rod of iron which (thanks be to the mercy of our God!) is placed in the hand of Him to whom all judgment is committed. The words therefore imply nothing as to the ultimate issue. But a deep truth is suggested by them. Do we speak quite accurately when we talk about sins being forgiven? It is surely the sinner rather than the sin that is forgiven; and this is what we really mean. The sin is cast off and cast out, condemned, and abolished. This is clearly the meaning of the word 'remission' in the Nicene Creed. God can never make terms with any sin. His wrath

---

[1] See Eph. ii. 7.

abides on it ; it is eternally doomed. It is sometimes forgotten that there is another sin clearly shown to be unpardonable by the very words with which our Master taught His disciples to pray—the sin of refusing to forgive a brother who has wronged us.

There is one passage, and I think only one, that seems to me to present a very serious difficulty to those who contend for the doctrine of a universal recovery and deliverance ; it is the text in which our Lord, apparently referring to Judas, says, ' it had been well (καλὸν) for that man if he had not been born.' I am familiar with several interpretations of that text advanced by the advocates of Restitution, but I cannot honestly say that any one of them so entirely commends itself to my mind as to enforce conviction. But the shuddering terror which such words are calculated to inspire is to a great extent mitigated when we listen attentively to those other words from the same lips, ' None of them is lost but the son of perdition, that the Scripture might be fulfilled.' For an expression so remarkable challenges attention, and the thought is at once suggested—it is ' the son of perdition ' (or, as S. Paul would say, ' the old Adam ') in Judas that is doomed and lost, and not till that is brought about can Judas himself be found and restored. And then those other words make their music heard, ' The Father loveth the Son, and hath

given all things into His hand,'[1] followed by 'All that
the Father giveth Me shall come to Me; and him
that cometh to Me I will in no wise cast out.'[2]

I cannot pursue this portion of my subject further.
I will only add that, whatever seeming difficulties and
contradictions there may be in the Bible, it is the
Book of the God of Hope, and is itself the Gospel of
Hope, and by Hope we are saved.[3] They who believe
in the Incarnation because they believe in the Bible,
whose faith rests on a Book, not on a Person, are not
inconsistent, however unreasonable, if, finding words
here and there in their oracle that seem to attribute
permanence to man's rebellion, and to teach a future
torment as endless as it is profitless, they declare it to
be a revealed truth. But Catholics, believing in the
Bible because they believe in the Incarnation, and
building on Christ, both God and man, as the only
foundation, are surely inconsistent if, in deference to
a few texts variously interpreted, and forgetful of the
many passages which seem clearly to support another

---

[1] S. John iii. 35. [2] *Ibid.* vi. 37.

[3] 'What is on the surface of the Bible is the way in which from
first to last it is one unbroken, persistent call to Hope.'—R. W. Church :
Advent Sermons, p. 91. Surely there is truth capable of wide appli-
cation in what Faber says about the Saints : 'They look at sinners as
saints themselves in possibility. Their hopefulness is the secret of their
charity. . . . Thus it is that apostolic zeal, with its enlightened love,
looks at sinners as the materials for the future triumphs of Jesus, as the
harvest yet ungarnered of His Passion.'—*The Creator and the Creature*,
p. 374.

conclusion, forgetful also of the testimony of the other witnessing voices which are always entitled at least to respectful consideration in the council-chambers of the Church—Catholic tradition and Christian philosophy—they venture to introduce definitions and limitations which the Church in her inspired wisdom and charity has never sanctioned. By her baptismal and eucharistic creeds her children are bound, and by their very obligations their liberties are protected. It is becoming increasingly clear, I think, year by year that the Catholic Symbols are our most effectual and enduring safeguard against narrowness, one-sidedness, and the tyranny of unauthorised and unverified theological opinions, so often loudly insisted upon, under the pressure of heated controversy, by contending ecclesiastical parties. Christ, Whom the creeds reveal, is Himself the Living Truth, and in Him we are empowered to ascend by a 'new and living way' to those 'heavenly places' where speculation is meditation, an activity of the spirit whereby 'the eyes of the heart' are enlightened, and a ladder securely planted upon which the angels of aspiration, ascending and descending, spread and fold their wings. It is to souls so exercised, far removed from the strife of tongues, and tasting habitually the sweetness of the 'hidden manna' of the Word, that this gospel of Restitution seems from age to age to commend itself, and never once has the voice of the Church been raised in condemnation of so encouraging, so stimulating a hope.[1]

But I must not tarry in this perfumed chamber of the great temple, wherein the upsoaring aspiration of Christian mysticism does so much to illuminate truth and to soften the hardness of religious controversy.

(3) With regard to patristic teaching on Eschatology, I am content to refer my readers to the numerous passages cited by Dr. Pusey, Mr. Jukes, the Dean of Wells, and others. It is easy, no doubt, to produce a long list of authorities on one side of the controversy, and a comparatively short one on the other ; but the latter will be found to include names of great weight, and they appear to speak, for the most part, without hesitation or embarrassment, their teaching exciting neither surprise nor suspicion. This is specially true of S. Gregory of Nyssa, who more than any other father is responsible for the concluding articles appended to the Nicene Creed at Constantinople. ‘What Origen whispered to the ear in the secret chamber,’ says Dean Plumptre, ‘was proclaimed by

[1] I have in my mind, among many others, the case of the Mother Juliana, a devout anchorite of Norwich, who lived in the 14th century. In her sixteen Revelations of the Love of God, so full of tenderness, penetration, fervour, and spiritual insight, she repeatedly speaks of a restoration that shall embrace all men.

Gregory of Nyssa as from the housetop. His universalism is as wide and unlimited as that of Bishop Newton of Bristol.' And again, 'What is noticeable in Gregory of Nyssa is that, in thus teaching, there is no apparent consciousness that he is deviating into the bye-paths of new and strange opinions. He claims to be taking his stand on the doctrines (δόγματα) of the Church in thus teaching, with as much confidence as when he is expounding the mysteries of the Divine Nature as set forth in the Creed of Nicæa. And the same absence of any sense of being even in danger of heresy is seen in most of those who followed in his footsteps, or those of Origen.' [1]

There is a formidable difficulty, much insisted on by those who maintain the commonly accepted doctrine, which certainly demands very careful and patient consideration, the freedom of the will. All are agreed that God will not and cannot coerce the will; to do so would be to violate the law by which He rules His rational creatures, and to make their obedience morally valueless. But how can we be sure, it is urged, that wills disobedient here and now will ever cease to be disobedient? All experience is against it, for habit forms character, and character stiffens and hardens with time. The objection can only be

[1] P. 140.

met, I think, by abandoning the appeal to experience
in deference to revelation. It is only on the high
spiritual plane that the argument can be answered.
To the children of faith it will not seem irrational if
we reply : Whatever our experience under these conditions may be, the conclusion to which it points
must be precarious when we are speaking of life
under conditions wholly different. It would surely
be presumptuous to assert that the inventiveness of
Divine Compassion is of necessity exhausted on this
side the grave. When the scales fall from our eyes—

> 'And then as, mid the dark, a gleam
> Of yet another morning breaks,
> And like the hand which ends a dream,
> Death, with the might of his sunbeam,
> Touches the flesh and the soul awakes '—[1]

then, in the awakening rapture of that sunrise, it is
at least conceivable that the vision grows brighter
and clearer, and that the revealed beauty of God,
though He be a consuming fire—nay, because He is a
consuming fire—may, without constraining the will, yet
exercise such a legitimate attraction that all will be
sooner or later won to the acknowledgment of His
claim upon their obedience.[2] We are too apt to

[1] Browning.

[2] 'The merits of Jesus reach to every soul who wills to be saved,
whether in this life they knew Him or knew Him not.'—Pusey, *E.P.*
p. 23.

forget that things impossible with men are possible
with God. And it should not be forgotten that in
our sin-disabled condition the freedom of the will is
from the first necessarily and seriously impaired ; it
is not really a free agent until it is established in
divine grace, and perfectly at one with the originating
Will, the Father-Will whose child it is. For our Lord
has said, 'every one that committeth sin is the bond-
servant of sin.'[1] This inherited infirmity of the will,
limiting, until it is healed, its freedom, is too often
ignored.

Another objection very commonly urged against
the doctrine of the Restitution of all is, I think, from
the Christian standpoint, quite inadmissible. It is
said that such a doctrine must tend to laxity, and, if
generally accepted, prove demoralising. Does not
such an objection betray the spirit of the early
rigorists and puritans—Montanists, Novatians, and
others—who condemned what they considered the
dangerous laxity of the Catholic Church in granting
absolution to grievous offenders on evidence of sincere
repentance ? The truth is, all spiritual truth is fraught
with peril in the hands of carnal men. The liber-
alities of God's pardoning grace will ever be to them
a reason for continuing in sin. But when once the
heart begins to respond to the love of God, they

[1] S. John viii. 34.

become a constraining motive for true and generous repentance. It cannot, I think, be doubted that many are postponing repentance at this hour, because the commonly received teaching about hell appears to them inconsistent with Divine love and justice.[1]

But there are one or two objections that may with much reason be brought forward on the other side. Among many of those who reject the doctrine of a universal Restitution, a tendency discovers itself which, if it be insisted on and consistently carried out, leads to a conclusion certainly heretical. Just as an extreme party in the Roman Church assigns the Kingdom of Justice to Christ, that of Mercy to Mary, and among Calvinists the still more serious error obtains of attributing Mercy to the Son, Justice to the Father, and representing the work of Christ to be, not the revelation of the Father's Will by fulfilling it, but the altering of that Will, subverting the doctrine of the Divine Unity; so in like manner the popular

---

[1] It has been urged, and not without reason, that 'a partial salvation plays into the hands of sin, and is a weapon of the evil power.' And again, 'While men take their stand upon sin as the reality, and indicate the hope merely as a possibility, they strengthen the hold of sin upon mankind, and smother the capacities which the hope would have awakened in the love of truth and horror of sin' (*Letters from a Mystic of the Present Day*,' p. 24). But the writer needs perhaps to be reminded that S. Augustine represents the mind of the Church when he refuses to recognise in sin anything substantial.

teaching on Eschatology, so often and so ignorantly called ' orthodox,' is constantly guilty of a similar offence, 'dividing the substance' of God by marshalling one attribute against another, whereas it is part of the alphabet of Catholic theology that the attributes are substantial characteristics which belong to the very nature of God, so that no one attribute can be exercised apart from the others, much less can any two be brought into conflict.[1]   Love is the name given to that which includes all.   It follows, therefore, that His wrath is His love ; it is the form love of necessity takes when dealing with sin ; and in like manner mercy would cease to be mercy if it failed to be justice ; and justice, if forgetful of mercy, would be injustice.   Our 'God is a consuming fire ' ; and the fire cannot but burn up the hay, wood, stubble ; cannot but refine the precious metal.   What is needed is not a less austere, but a more austere teaching.   The Church will surely fail in her mission if, knowing ' the

[1] ' It is true that His several attributes, as our finite minds are compelled to regard them, are not really distinct, but one with Himself, and are merged in His adorable Simplicity' : Oxenham, *Catholic Eschatology*—a book containing much that I can heartily endorse, but written in a somewhat bitter controversial tone, and lacking, as it seems to me, theological depth and grasp—like so many books of controversy, clever rather than conclusive.   From one whose *Catholic Doctrine of the Atonement* was a really valuable contribution to theology, something stronger, calmer, and of more permanent value might have been expected on the subject under discussion.   But I am unwilling to criticise the work of an old friend.

terrors of the Lord,'[1] she does not seek by them to persuade men. But the terrors of the Lord are not to make cowards, but heroes, of us ; it is not salutary pain or needful punishment that we are to fear, but sin—its treason to the love of God, its base ingratitude, its sacrilegious desecration of that which His goodness has sanctified. It is the 'goodness' of His 'longsuffering and forbearance' that leads us to repentance. His terrors are persuasive because they carry with them a revelation of His tenderness.[2]

The popular teaching about hell is not austere ; it is not even awful ; it may scare children ; it does not solemnise men. In truth, it does nothing but obscure the really awful, reasonable, and salutary doctrine of hell.[3] 'Where the worm dieth not, and the fire is not quenched.' These are awful words certainly, if, with S. Jerome, we understand the 'fire' and 'worm' to signify memory and conscience ; but if the lot of those who so suffer were hopeless, I cannot but think that suffering of that kind would of necessity cease ; it is not the utterly and hopelessly

---

[1] 2 Cor. v. 11.   [2] Rom. ii. 4.

[3] 'Was there no connection between the denial of hell and its semi-realisation upon earth for a brief space during the Reign of Terror in Paris ?' (Cazenove). I think there was ; but the same history may serve to remind us also how little good can come of a 'reign of terror,' like that which popular Eschatology has sometimes sought to establish upon earth.

hardened conscience, but the conscience awakened to self-abhorrence and penitence that suffers.

Hell itself (thank God !) can only come to an end when those things utterly perish which, so long as they exist, must have their place in hell—pride, envy, greed, selfishness, and all the sinful lusts both of the flesh and of the spirit.[1] If hell exists everlastingly, we may be sure it is no less for the vindication of God's love than of His righteousness.   But, I confess, Revelation xx. 14 seems to me to point to a different conclusion.

Again, one thing is constantly forgotten in this controversy ; the purpose of Revelation is not to reveal the future, but to reveal God, to unveil His Countenance, to make us acquainted with His Character.   Knowing Him, we know not only that all is well, but that all is best.   Can we not trust One Who is a Faithful Creator and most Merciful Saviour— One Whose Name is Love, Whose Life, Sacrifice ?   Is not this enough ?   Are we not guilty of self-seeking,

---

[1] This is surely one of the many things that give to Dante's majestic poem such a permanent theological value, its witness to the wrath of God abiding on sin, to the meaning and necessity of Divine Retribution, as well as of Purification and Beatitude.   The question is whether that not to be evaded and altogether necessary punishment does not in the end separate between the sin and the sinner, and liberate the latter by abolishing the former.   The great Florentine once or twice makes use of words which seem to imply that in his judgment such a hope is not inadmissible.

as well as of distrust, inconsistent with the true spirit
of sonship, if we allow ourselves to be clouded or
embarrassed by perplexities or uncertainties about
our future destiny? Is it not a subtle form of that
'other worldliness' which is in a child of God nothing
less than criminal inconsistency? What we know of
Him forbids us, I humbly submit, to believe in a
perpetuity of evil. If hell be everlasting, may we not
be sure that it is one of the 'many mansions' in which
His righteousness will be everlastingly vindicated, and
the glory of His love everlastingly revealed?

This conclusion is certainly supported by the
accepted Roman teaching about the destiny of lost
souls, indicated by the words 'refrigeria,' 'mitigatio,'
'respiratio.' Cardinal Newman, in the 'Grammar of
Assent,' has called attention to some remarkable
words of Petavius, in which he says that the Catholic
Church has left the question an open one, and implies
that the milder view was entertained by the Fathers.[1]

Newman, with that characteristic humility which
is, indeed, the truest sagacity, concludes by submit-
ting the whole question to the Theological School.

It has been publicly stated by Dr. Cazenove, an
able defender of the doctrine of everlasting punishment, that Père Ravignan and the Jesuits are disposed to go much farther in the direction of Univer-

[1] P. 417.

salism. I have had no means of verifying the asser-
tion, but it is one which will not greatly surprise those
who are acquainted with the theological tendencies of
the celebrated Company.

Among modern English writers on this momentous
question there are three whose words are to my mind
weighty and deserving of special and very serious
attention—Mr. Maurice, Canon Westcott, and Dean
Church. In a controversy that has called forth on
both sides so much reckless and shallow writing, it is
a relief to turn to teaching so calm, so searching, and
so inspiring as theirs. The testimony of Mr. Maurice
is specially valuable, for he was brought up a Univer-
salist, deliberately rejected his inherited opinion as his
mind matured, and never returned to it. To him,
however, the austerest of teachers, it was given, more
perhaps than to any other man, to recommend the
larger hope. His ripe convictions on this subject are
to be found in a long letter to Professor Hort, a letter
which contains an earnest and powerful vindication
of the Athanasian Creed, and concludes with some
beautiful words on the Eucharistic Sacrifice. The
following are the conclusions at which he arrives :—

‘ My duty I feel is this : (1) To assert that which
I know, that which God has revealed, His absolute,
universal love in all possible ways, and without any
limitation. (2) To tell myself and all men that to

know this love and to be moulded by it is the blessing we are to seek. (3) To say that this is eternal life (4) To say that the want of it is death. (5) To say that if they believe in the Son of God they have eternal life. (6) To say that if they have not the Son of God they have not life. (7) Not to say who has the Son of God, because I do not know. (8) Not to say how long anyone may remain in eternal death, because I do not know. (9) Not to say that all will necessarily be raised out of eternal death, because I do not know. (10) Not to judge any before the time, or to judge other men at all, because Christ has said, "Judge not, that ye be not judged." (11) Not to play with Scripture by quoting passages which have not the slightest connection with the subject, such as, "Where the tree falleth, it shall lie." (12) Not to invent a scheme of purgatory, and so take upon myself the office of the Divine Judge. (13) Not to deny God a right of using punishments at any time or anywhere for the reformation of His creatures. (14) Not to contradict Christ's words, "Those shall be beaten with few, these with many stripes," for the sake of maintaining a theory of the equality of sins. (15) Not to think any punishment of God's so great as His saying, "Let them alone." '[1]

In another letter he says, 'I cannot believe that God

[1] *Life of F. D. M.* vol. ii. p. 20.

will fail with any at last ; if the work was in any other hands it might be wasted, but His Will must surely be done, however long it may be resisted.'[1] And again, ' I have desired, and hope always to desire, for myself and all men, that we may never cease to be punished by God till we cease to punish ourselves by rebelling against Him.'[2]

' Men are awakened to the sense of their own evil —of a tormenting self. They hear of a Saviour to whom they can fly from themselves, of a Father who is seeking after them. They begin to believe in an eternal home in a Father's House ; and that from which they fly is hell—the torment of the worm in their conscience, the misery of being left alone with themselves. That is the eternal death from which they cry to be delivered. They take no measure of its continuance. It is with them. It is now. It darkens all the past ; it throws its horror over the future. O God, Thou hast been a refuge from it throughout all generations. Thou wilt be our refuge from it thoroughout the generations to come. Punish us as Thou wilt. Punish us, if it please Thee to do so, for ever. But keep us from this death. Raise us out of it. Unite us to that Life which is in Thee, and which, except in Thee, we can never possess.'[3]

[1] Vol. ii. p. 575.   [2] Vol. ii. p. 342.
[3] Vol. ii. p. 476.

In his admirable book on 'The Historic Faith'
Canon Westcott writes as follows concerning the concluding article of the Apostles' Creed :—

'We declare our belief in the "life eternal"—that
is, faith's proclamation of the fulness of the divine
victory—and we go no farther. Yet we cannot
wholly suppress the questions which arise when we
pronounce words full of the largest hope. Does this
life exclude death wholly and in all its forms? Does
it include that "restitution of all things" which is proposed as the aim of human repentance and effort?
Or does it leave room for existences finally alien from
God, and unsubdued by His love, for evil, as evil, enduring as God is? To suggest this last alternative
seems to be to admit the possibility of a dualism in a
form wholly inconceivable. The present existence of
evil carries with it difficulties to which nature offers
no solution ; but to suppose that evil once introduced
into the world is for ever, appears to be at variance
with the essential conception of God as revealed
to us.

'There may, however, be some fallacy in our
way of conceiving and stating these questions. We
know too little of the purifying and consuming fire of
God's love, too little of the effect of punishment when
it is seen in the spiritual completeness of perfect
justice, too little of our corporate union one with

another in virtue of our common humanity, to be able
to form theories as to the world to come. And
Scripture does not encourage us to enter on such an
effort. The reserve of the prophetic and apostolic
writings as to the unseen world is as remarkable as
the boldness with which uninspired teachers have pre-
sumed to deal with it.

'But two thoughts bearing upon the future find
clear expression in the New Testament. The one is
the consequences of unrepented sin as answering to
the sin ; the other of a final unity in which God shall
be all in all. We read of an "eternal sin," of "a sin
which has no forgiveness in this world nor in the
world to come," of a debt incurred of which the pay-
ment to be rigidly exacted exceeds all imaginable
resources of the debtor, of "eternal destruction," of
"the worm that dieth not and the fire that is not
quenched." And on the other side we read of the
purpose, the good pleasure of God, "to sum up all
things in Christ," and "through Him to reconcile all
things unto Himself, whether things upon the earth
or things in the heavens," of the bringing to naught
of the last enemy death, and the final subjection of all
things to God.

'Moreover, it must be added, these apparently
antithetical statements correspond with two modes of
regarding the subject from the side of reason. If we

approach it from the side of man, we see that in themselves the consequences of actions appear to be for the doer, like the deed, indelible; and also that the finite freedom of the individual appears to include the possibility of final resistance to God. And again, if we approach it from the Divine side, it seems to be an inadmissible limitation of the infinite love of God that a human will should for ever refuse to yield to it in complete self-surrender when it is known as love.

'If we are called upon to decide which of these two lines of reasoning, which of these two thoughts of Scripture must be held to prevail, we can hardly doubt that that which is the most comprehensive, that which reaches farthest, contains the ruling idea : and that is the idea of a final divine unity. How it will be reached we are wholly unable to say ; but we are sure that the manner, which has not been revealed, will be in perfect harmony with the justice of God and the obligations of man's responsibility. More than this we dare not lay down. But that end—"the end"—rises before us as the strongest motive and the most certain encouragement in all the labours of the life of faith.' [1]

'Let us submit,' writes the Dean of St. Paul's, 'to the conditions of our state and of our knowledge ; we,

[1] *The Historic Faith*, pp. 149-151.

at least, who in the tempests and confusions of the
world have as our supreme guiding light the manifestation, the words, of the Son of God.   Who shall
say that, though we must greatly fear, we may not
also greatly hope, even if we are met by awful certain-
ties, if we dare not say more than He has said?   We
cannot tell what is between the grave and the judgment; but we know that the living God is there, very
terrible, very pitiful, very just, Who leads His creatures
by ways they know not, to the end which only He
knows.   We may be sure that He will set right in
His own way the inequalities of the world.   We may
be sure that all who seek Him in truth shall one day
find Him, for He has said so.   We may be sure that
every one in every nation who feareth Him and worketh
righteousness is accepted with Him, for His accredited
Apostle has said so.   Is the righteousness of God too
small a thing to trust to, unless we can say in detail
how it is to be carried out?   Are "the multitude of
His mercies," to use a favourite phrase of the Psalms—
the multitude of His mercies, to which saint and penitent must alike appeal—are they too stinted, too
straitened, that we cannot commit to them all the
infinite issues of human life which move our fellow-
feeling, our pity, our sympathy?   Can we be so com-
passionate and so just, and cannot we trust Him to
be so, unless He shows us how?   Can we not trust

Him, in silent and awful expectation, with the work
of His own hands, sure that He will not despise it,
sure that under the shadow of His wings all the
countless multitude of His creatures, from the highest
to the lowest, the worst and the best, shall find His
perfect truth, sure that each soul will receive what it
ought to receive, and will be dealt with by infinite
goodness and unerring justice.'[1]

Such is the conclusion of a masterly sermon on
'Sin and Judgment,' preached before the University
of Oxford by one who, if any man does, speaks with
authority, and commands the affectionate veneration
and entire confidence of all to whom the Catholic
Faith inherited by the Church of England is dear.
Under such guidance we may do more than 'faintly
trust the larger hope'; we may gladly and gratefully
bid it welcome, and seek more and more to know
its enkindling inspiration and its sanctifying power.

Thus it has been given to some of our later theologians to reassert the wider hope—the fuller gospel—
that was so familiar and so dear to not a few of the
early fathers of the Church. The faith which expressed itself in the worship of the Catacombs was not
...rely at fault when upon the shoulder of the Good

[1] *Human Life and its Conditions*, pp. 122-124. Glad indeed
should I be if I could persuade all my readers to make themselves
acquainted with this sermon—admirable no less for its searching and
tender severity than for the infinite hope that it suggests.

Shepherd it beheld, not a lamb, but a goat. The great poet who has just been taken from us discerned the meaning of that rude, but deeply significant picture, and in a sonnet, full of tender pathos, gave expression to the joy inseparable from the hope for the future of all men suggested by it, a joy which multitudes have felt, though they have often been half afraid to entertain it :—

> ' *He saves the sheep, the goats he doth not save !*
> So rang Tertullian's sentence, on the side
> Of that unpitying Phrygian sect which cried :
> " Him can no fount of fresh forgiveness lave,
>
> Who sins, once wash'd by the baptismal wave !'
> So spake the fierce Tertullian. But she sigh'd,
> The infant Church ; of love she felt the tide
> Stream on her from her Lord's yet recent grave.
>
> And then she smiled, and in the Catacombs,
> With eye suffused but heart inspired true,
> On those walls subterranean, where she hid
>
> Her head in ignominy, death, and tombs,
> She her Good Shepherd's hasty image drew ;
> And on his shoulders, not a lamb, a kid.'

My last quotation shall be from another poet whose voice is still stronger and sweeter, and whose testimony to Christ grows more earnest and emphatic with advancing years. His words on the subject of the ' larger hope ' express with a tender and delicate

reserve a lofty and intuitive aspiration. The verses
in 'In Memoriam' are well known and often quoted.
Less familiar, perhaps, are the concluding lines of the
' Vision of Sin ' :—

> 'At last I heard a voice upon the slope
> Cry to the summit, "Is there any hope?"
> To which an answer pealed from that high land,
> But in a tongue no man could understand :
> And on the glimmering limit far withdrawn
> God made Himself an awful rose of dawn.'

Does that imply suspense? I do not think so.
The poet feels the sunrise to be a more convincing
and satisfactory answer than any that lips could utter,
and the awfulness is felt by the poet-heart (oh, how
truly!) to be that of supreme and surpassing loveli-
ness—of all-penetrating, all-conquering light, with
which no darkness can for a moment compete.

Many, therefore, are the voices that throughout
the ages bear witness concerning the Divine Purpose,
the Spirit and the Bride speaking with one utterance,
and empowering others also to speak in the Name of
the Son of Man. But there are two chosen witnesses
whose testimony throughout the ages is of supreme
importance ; S. John speaks of them as ' the Water '
and ' the Blood.'[1] It is the Water of Purification and the
Blood of Sacrifice (that is, of spiritual vitality), and both

[1] 1 John v. 8.

are the ministers of Life. In Genesis the River of Life is a fourfold stream encompassing the world; in the vision of Ezekiel it is seen to flow from beneath the altar of God's Temple, a sacrificial river whose sweet waters heal the bitterness of the salt sea waters of Death ; and in the Apocalypse that mystic stream mirrors in its crystal depths the foliage and the fruitage of the recovered Tree of Life, whose roots it feeds, and whose interlacing boughs (for it grows on either bank) overarch it, the lovely canopy of a Heavenly Font. The leaves of that Tree, we are told, 'are for the healing of the nations.'

But still more clear and penetrating is the witnessing voice of the divine Chalice of the Eucharist, for the Life is in the Blood, and the Blood shed is the Life surrendered, not that it may be wasted and lost, but that it may be effectually communicated, and become through sacramental ministry the life-blood of the Bride and the children of the Bride-chamber. 'Drink ye all of it,' says throughout the ages the voice of the consecrated and consecrating Priest, Who having loved His own loves them unto the end—surely an endless end—and Who came that we might have life, and have it more abundantly.

But the Church's testimony, expressing an invincible, inextinguishable hope for all her children, has other modes of utterance enforcing that of her two chosen, sacramental witnesses. The Psalter is the bundle of myrrh between her breasts, dear to her heart, the inspired expression of her highest and most dearly cherished aspirations, the perpetual music that accompanies her endless Eucharistic Feast ; and the Psalter is full of the largest hopes for the redemption of the whole universe ; the doctrine of the Restitution of all things runs through it like a golden thread.

And, once more, the Lord's Prayer, which is in one sense her only prayer, and of which her every Liturgy is but an expansion, can hardly, as it seems to me, be intelligently used by those who reject this doctrine. For in it her children are taught to say, ' Thy Will be done on earth, as it is in heaven.' Now, what God's Will is concerning His children is by no means uncertain. He wills that all men should be saved and come to a knowledge of the Truth ; and that that Will is perfectly fulfilled in heaven the petition He has Himself put upon our lips distinctly asserts. How then can that petition be a real prayer, faithfully and intelligently presented by us at the Throne of Grace, unless it is accompanied by a conviction concerning human destiny that is irreconcilable with the persuasion that His Holy Will is destined to be eternally crossed by sin, and by sinners His saving Purpose eternally frustrated ?

Such considerations as these, it will be said, are

D

precarious and inconclusive. I do not deny it. Nor
would I dwell upon them in the presence of a well-
sustained theological conclusion, much less of an
authoritative decision, on the other side; but in the
absence of either they may, I think, be legitimately
pressed on the attention of all who, in the solution
of a great problem, are anxious before all things to
ascertain the mind of the Church.

The theory of annihilation or conditional immor-
tality is one which I do not care to discuss, for I am
persuaded that it will never commend itself to the
mind and heart and conscience of the Spirit-bearing
and Spirit-guided Church. A few men, both earnest
and able, in ancient and in modern times, have
adopted it. I cannot think they would have done
so, had they not been driven into it as a way of
escape from the popular teaching about hell, and
under the impression that the gospel of Restitution
is too good to be true. But, God being what He is,
nothing can be too good to be true; the better it is,
the more likely to be His truth, Who is ever devising
means whereby His banished ones may be restored.
I am content, therefore, to pass by the discussion of
this theory, endorsing the indictment of one of the
calmest and most sagacious writers on Eschatology.
The Dean of Wells says of annihilation—'Whatever
support that view may derive from a narrow and

almost slavish literalism in its interpretation of Scripture, it must be rejected as at variance with the intuitive beliefs which all God's later revelation presupposes, at variance also with the meaning of Scripture when we pass beyond the letter to the truths which it represents.'[1] He might, I think, have added that it is this view, and not that of Restitution, which is calculated to promote laxity; for it addresses itself to that which is mean and unworthy in human nature, man's desire at any cost to avoid suffering, whereas the other doctrine makes appeal to that which is lofty and generous, a conviction that good is in the end stronger than evil and destined to overcome it, and that the one thing from which we need to be delivered at any cost of suffering is sin.

It cannot, I think, be questioned that the oft-repeated appeal to fear—not the fear of God, not the fear of sin, but the fear of pain—has a demoralising effect both on those who make and those who accept it. It is not the method of the Master and His Apostles. Love is ever rebuking selfishness and putting it to shame, not by denunciations and penalties, but by bearing, believing, hoping, and enduring all things, discerning in every offender one who is overtaken in a fault, and knows not what he does.[2]

May I venture, before I conclude, to say a word

[1] P. 16.   [2] Gal. vi. 1; S. Luke xxiii. 34.

or two to those who go along with me in this matter? It is surely our duty to stand aloof from, and, when occasion offers, to protest against, what goes by the name of Universalism. The word has a good meaning, no doubt, like Gnosticism, Puritanism, and many more, but it has been fatally discredited by a party whose theory is tainted with rationalism, and its practice with laxity. We shall be wise, however, if, while contending earnestly, as I believe we are bound to do, against the errors of Universalists, we are careful to do justice to that element of truth which alone gives to their contention its force and spiritual vitality. 'Errors,' as Hinton has reminded us, 'are so many sign-posts, saying "the truth lies out there."' And we shall do well, I am persuaded, to insist on the distinction between the pollution of sin and its penal consequences, and to make it quite plain that it is not the doctrine of everlasting punishment that we call in question, but that of everlasting sin—of God's perpetual defeat by the success of a permanent rebellion against Him on the part of a section of His family—yes, though it be the persistent defiance of but one of His children. It has often seemed to me that, far from contradicting the belief in universal Restoration, the doctrine of eternal punishment rather points to it.[1]

[1] In making this suggestion I am glad to find myself in agreement with the Dean of Wells. He says, 'Strange as the paradox may seem,

Being sinners, we can, uncondemned and unpunished, know no salvation; and it may well be that that punishment and condemnation must endure if our salvation is to be secured and perfected.

To those who differ from me I would say in all loving earnestness, Consider calmly in the way of systematic meditation the texts to which you appeal as opposed to the gospel of Restitution, and see whether, interrogated in this way, they do not yield a very different meaning from that which has been vulgarly associated with them. And ask yourselves whether you can seriously call in question any one of the following statements :—

1. Large tracts of Holy Scripture seem clearly to sanction and enforce the doctrine you reject.

2. Great saints and doctors have earnestly believed and fearlessly proclaimed it.

3. The Church of England almost immediately recalled the 42nd Article, introduced under Puritan influence, that condemned it.

4. The Church Catholic, although the controversy has been before her since the days of Origen, has never closed it by an authoritative decision.[1]

the belief even in a universal restoration is compatible with a belief also in the eternity of punishment.'—*The Spirits in Prison*, p. 353.

[1] We have no evidence that the belief in the ἀποκατάστασις ('restitution'), which prevailed in the fourth and fifth centuries, was ever definitely condemned by any council of the Church.—*The Spirits in Prison*, p. 141. See Appendix.

It is a Catholic principle from which, if we be Churchmen, there is no appeal, that the Church is above both individuals and parties, and that in her silence, no less than in her utterance, she is under a Divine guidance and control. Let us, therefore, one and all, not permit ourselves to forget what is an undisputed, though often violated, axiom and a binding rule : Not to condemn what the Church has refrained from condemning, and not to force on the acceptance of others what she has never insisted on as *de fide*. As with the doctrines of Inspiration and the Atonement, so with regard to Retribution also she has wisely and charitably abstained from definitions which were not needed, and it is not competent to any of her children to impugn the wisdom of her comprehensiveness, to disallow her hopes, or to dwarf her creed. If the sobriety of an accurate and profound theological science be habitually preferred to the extravagance that too often disfigures the rhetoric of the pulpit, there is not, I apprehend, much to fear. It is the happy destiny of light to conquer darkness, and all who love the light and come to it shall be gathered ultimately into the Unity of the Truth. Already I cannot but believe that a higher and stronger position than that commonly taken by English Churchmen in the past is within our reach, and is being, I rejoice to know, increasingly occupied

by those who have the best title to the name of
Catholic. If called upon to engage in controversy,
let us never forget that the controversial spirit is a
defiling presence in the sanctuary of Truth, and that
here, as elsewhere, Love is the only Potentate, the
only Conqueror. Who that has ever entered the lists
does not know how hard it is in the conflict of words
not to belittle, even if we do not pervert, the truth?

The doctrine of Restitution, if I am not mistaken,
will be increasingly accepted by the 'children of the
Resurrection,' as the Church's apprehension of four
mysteries, under the guidance of the Spirit of Wisdom,
gradually deepens :—

(1) Our Lord's Descent into hell.

(2) The unity of the dual spheres of Love, of which
relationship and attribute are respectively the distin-
guishing features, in the ever-developing Life of the
Mystical Body.

(3) The obligation of the Church, 'in the Regene-
ration,' to justify her election by perpetuating in her
perfected conformity a sacrificial ministry.

(4) The Priesthood of Melchizedek, whereby in
the final consummation the non-elect shall be accepted,
sealed, and consecrated.

In the meantime the Church finds her strength in
quietness and confidence, in faith and patience; anti-
cipating, with the dauntless hope that her age-long

experience of God's Faithfulness inspires, the victorious manifestation of that Dayspring from on high, when a great Voice out of heaven shall make proclamation : ' Behold, the Tabernacle of God is with men, and He will dwell with them, and they shall be His people, and God Himself shall be with them, and be their God. And God shall wipe away all tears from their eyes ; and there shall be no more death, neither sorrow, nor crying, neither shall there be any more pain : for the former things are passed away.' [1]

And now to sum up and conclude. Up to a certain point all who are not in bondage to the Calvinistic tradition will, I think, be agreed ; and when the point is reached at which we shall have to agree to differ, we shall, I believe, be very much mistaken if we attach to our differences the importance which, in the heat of controversy, has been attributed to them by disputants on either side.

1. We shall all be agreed that God changes not ; that always and everywhere His tender mercies are over all His works ; that His Name is Love, a Name that is never belied, a Love that can never forsake.

2. That He is of too pure eyes to look upon iniquity, and can make no compromise with sin.

3. That no judgment or action of His is ever capricious or vindictive.

[1] Apoc. xxi. 3, 4.

4. That the Self-sacrifice, involved in the Incarnation and Passion of Christ, does not change His Will, but reveals and fulfils it—declares it to be unchanging, by the which Will all are saved and sanctified.[1]

5. That, respecting the freedom of His children, He will never coerce them, but will not cease to follow them when they wander, with the unwearied pursuit of His parental solicitude, since charity bears all things and never fails, never tires of overcoming evil with good, of heaping coals of fire in ever-renewed lovingkindness on the heads of those who perversely oppose themselves.

6. That His calling and election are without repentance ; and that man's repentance is always a response to the call of His prevenient grace.

7. That His forgiveness always and everywhere waits upon and rewards repentance.

8. That the plenteous redemption wrought by Christ is a universal redemption by which the world is saved ; so that Christ is the Head of a redeemed and atoned Humanity, and the Saviour of all men, specially of those that believe.[2]

9. That the Church's witness is for the conviction, and her election for the salvation, of the world.

10. That sin is its own punishment, and the sinner of necessity under condemnation (damned).

---

[1] 1 Tim. ii. 4 ; Heb. x. 10.   [2] 1 Tim. iv. 10.

11. That the Christian conception of heaven is not enjoyment, nor that of hell torment.[1] We know not what we shall be, but we know that when He shall appear we shall be like Him, for we shall see Him as He is. It is a Beatific Vision of which the Church testifies, a vision that of necessity exercises a conforming power, and constrains those who behold it to live a life of love-inspired sympathy, service, sacrifice, to become priests and victims both for God and man. This is the heavenly life, because the Christ-life, whose highest beatitude is not getting, but giving. And hell is the forfeiture of this, involving the loss of all the precious blessings and dignities and capacities for service that are the heritage of the Firstborn—a veritable ' pœna damni.'

12. That salvation is not deliverance from the punishment, but from the pollution of sin.

So far I venture to hope we are all agreed.

The disagreement will probably discover itself if I go on to say—

1. That there seems to me to be nothing in Scripture or Catholic Tradition, as interpreted by the Creeds and Liturgies of the Church, that forbids us to believe that this world is not the only scene, or this life the only stage, of man's probation [2];

[1] Such a conception belongs to Islam, not to Christianity.

[2] Martensen examines the problem before us with all his accustomed penetration at the conclusion of his great work on *Christian*

nothing that obliges us, as a matter of loyalty to revealed truth, to forego the 'larger hope,' a hope which seems to be directly countenanced by large portions of Holy Scripture, and specially by our Lord's own most emphatic words about the ultimate success of that supreme attraction whereby He will in the end subdue all things to Himself.

2. That His Words also clearly encourage us to believe that there will be many gradations and varieties of spiritual condition among those who are excluded from His immediate Presence, since it will be more tolerable, He tells us, for some than for others in the Day of Judgment, and some will deserve 'many,' others 'few stripes.'[1]

3. That the Scriptural and Catholic doctrine of Election, which pervades the whole Bible and is briefly expressed by S. Paul's twice repeated words, 'a little leaven leaveneth the whole lump,' points to the

---

Dogmatics. He represents it to be one which the Church is not yet in a position to solve. He acknowledges that 'we are unable to harmonise the idea of eternal damnation with the Teleology of Divine Love' (p. 481). Discussing the question ' whether there be a *terminus peremptorius* for human conversion, *i.e.* an utmost limit beyond which true repentance and conversion are no longer possible,' he says, ' We dare not venture to fix this limit arbitrarily at any point within the course of time (*e.g.* at the end of this life)'; but he adds, ' We are unconditionally compelled to fix it at the end of time and history, and this corresponds exactly with the idea of the final advent of our Lord. While time lasts conversion must be possible' (p. 478).

[1] S. Luke xii. 47, 48.

ingathering of a completed harvest of Humanity, of which those who are in this dispensation incorporated into Christ are ' firstfruits.' [1]

4. That the words ' As in Adam all die, even so in Christ shall all be made alive,' seem to imply that for all men, whatever differences of condition there may be, there is ultimately but one destiny: a solidarity of mankind which would seem to be not only impaired, but destroyed, if any section of the human family is to remain for ever unreconciled.

5. That the enlightened reason and informed conscience of the Church have ever gladly welcomed and endorsed what would seem to be the least precarious of theological conclusions that are not matters of absolute certainty—namely, that evil, since it had a beginning, is destined to come to an end ; and that death and hell, emptied of their prey, their necessary and salutary work accomplished, shall be cast into the Lake of Fire, wherein all that is due to death dies, and all that is born of perdition is lost.[2] Then, at length, may the prophecy be fulfilled, ' There shall be no more curse ; ' and the promise be accomplished, ' Behold, I make all things new ; ' and from new heavens and a new earth, recreated in righteousness, shall arise the triumph-song wherein the seer of the Apocalypse heard all creatures uniting : ' Blessing, and honour,

---

[1] 1 Cor. xv. 23 ; S. James i. 18.   [2] Apoc. xx. 14.

and glory, and power, be unto Him that sitteth upon the throne, and unto the Lamb for ever and ever.'[1]

When his soul refused comfort, the Psalmist asked the tremendous question : 'Will the Lord absent Himself for ever, and will He be no more entreated ? Is His mercy clean gone for ever, and is His promise come utterly to an end for evermore ? Hath God forgotten to be gracious, and will He shut up His lovingkindness in displeasure ?' The question is answered by a multitude that no man can number, who sing the New Song in the ' Queen City,' Jerusalem, the Mother of us all ; it is answered by the patient love of a Shepherd Who seeks till He finds the sheep that is lost ; it is answered by His Voice, from the plain and gracious meaning of Whose prophetic words there would seem to be no appeal : ' I, if I be lifted up from the earth, will draw all men unto Me.'[2]

[1] Apoc. v. 13.   [2] S. John xii. 32.

APPENDIX.

AN attempt has been made in the foregoing pages to appeal on behalf of the larger hope to theological principles and standards of doctrine to which the respect of all Catholics is due. I have purposely abstained from any examination of the teaching and condemnation of Origen, and the history of the Fifth General Council. By the kindness of my friend, the Rev. H. H. Jeaffreson, this important and difficult matter is discussed, with a learning and ability beyond my power to command, in the following letter—a letter which is, I know, the outcome of much careful research and study, and, I venture to think, a contribution of permanent value to this momentous controversy, with which at present so many minds are occupied. To engage in it involves no small responsibility, and in undertaking it I cannot be sufficiently thankful for the encouraging sympathy and ready cooperation of so competent a scholar and so earnest a thinker.

'My Dear Gurney,—I heard with very great pleasure that you had been led to express in print some of those reasons which have moved you, as a Catholic priest, to espouse the hope that the final victory of our Redeemer over sin will be complete. The pleasure was increased when you kindly proposed that I should add to your essay a few words on the historical question, whether such a hope is in any way contradictory to any conciliar decision of the Catholic Church, or to the general testimony of her tradition as it is to be found in the Fathers. My pleasure is indeed alloyed by the consideration that you might easily have entrusted this important task to abler hands than mine ; but you could not have found any one who has investigated the matter with more scrupulous anxiety. For if the Church has indeed formulated any doctrine on the subject, I conceive that we are bound to accept it as the teaching of the Holy Spirit. My inquiry, then, has not been of a merely antiquarian character, but one which affected my whole conception of the Catholic Faith, in and by which I live, and hope to live.

'I shall restrict myself entirely to the historical question, leaving the scriptural and the philosophical departments of the inquiry in your abler hands.

'And first, let it be clearly stated that I hope to show, not that such a Restitution as we hope for is *de fide* but that it is left open for the acceptance of Catholics. I do not covet the luxury of calling those who differ from me heretics. Again, I do not wish to prove that every doctrine of Restitution is allowable : because some doctrines on the subject seem to me superficial, and some erroneous. Nor do I intend to concern myself with the question of everlasting punishment, but with that of everlasting sin. The latter is the fundamental question, the other secondary. If sin be everlasting, then assuredly must punishment be everlasting too. On the other hand, it does not follow that if sin be destined to eradication punishment will therefore cease. In this life we have abundance of instances of sin which, long after the sinner has repented of it and forsaken it, leaves its bitter penalty of suffering. Of injuries to the body, some, such as a scratch, are readily repaired, some, such as an amputation, are irreparable. It seems to me probable, in the way of analogy, that obstinate persistence in sin may so mutilate a man's spiritual faculties that he will never be such as he might have been had he not persisted in sin. If memory be anything, if there be no action in life which does not impress its stamp upon the total character, I cannot conceive that Nero will ever be as S. Paul, Voltaire as Fénelon. But my trust is that God will subdue to His obedience Nero and Voltaire and every sinner, so that no man shall for ever rebel against Him.

'My sole question, then, is this : Is there, either in the conciliar decrees of the Church, or in her general tradition, anything to forbid us to hope that,

E

in the end, God's truth shall prevail over the devil's lie in all men's minds, God's love triumph over selfishness in all hearts, so that He who is now the Saviour of them that believe shall bring all men into the obedience of faith, and be revealed as the Saviour of all men ?

'The matter is very closely connected with the question whether Origen has been condemned by the Church ; for if the doctrine of Restitution has been condemned it has been condemned in the person of Origen. But we must be on our guard against a two-fold assumption which pervades even Dr. Pusey's book on everlasting punishment. It is assumed that, if Origen was condemned, it was for his doctrine of Restitution ; and again, that, if his doctrine of Restitution was condemned, every other doctrine of Restitution was condemned with it. Whereas, if Origen was condemned, there were many other grounds of doctrine and discipline upon which his condemnation might be based ; and if his doctrine of Restitution was condemned, it is not the doctrine which we advocate, if indeed anyone advocates it at the present day. It was based upon his peculiar doctrine of pre-existence. In the beginning all rational creatures were one, equal, not individuated. In the exercise of free will these created spirits fell from God, some further, some less far : spirit was "chilled" into soul (a reference to a false derivation of $\psi v \chi \acute{\eta}$) and imprisoned in flesh, in which it should undergo discipline

until its sin was purged, and the whole rational creature should return to its pristine formless, incorporeal
unity. But, retaining the endowment of free will, the
rational creature remains for ever capable of a repeated
fall from God ; and therefore it is possible that the
history of all future ages will be one of repeated falls,
discipline, and restoration. Whether this is the real
doctrine of Origen or not (and on the whole I think it
is), this is at all events the doctrine usually attributed to
him in the Origenistic controversies, and therefore the
doctrine condemned in him. For instance, the Synod
of Constantinople in 541 (of which more hereafter) condemns not Restitution generally, but " the mythical
pre-existence of souls, and the prodigious restitution
which follows upon it." Such a condemnation no
more involves Restitution in general than Article XXII.
condemns all doctrines of Purgatory because it condemns the Romish doctrine about it.

‘ It is certain that Origen was condemned about
A.D. 231 by Demetrius of Alexandria and a synod of
" bishops and some priests," and that two years later
he was deposed by Demetrius in a provincial synod,
whose decrees were probably endorsed (according to
a popular custom of comity, which did not involve
independent inquiry into the case) at Rome and elsewhere. If these authorities could be shown to have
condemned, in the person of Origen, the doctrine for
which we plead, we should no doubt be bound to
listen to their verdict with respect, but not necessarily

to submit to it any more than to other provincial synods. But in fact the question is entirely open for what Origen was condemned. He had probably infringed the discipline of the Church by the rash act of his youth, and by seeking ordination in spite of it ; probably also by preaching while a layman, certainly by accepting holy orders at the hands of a bishop not his own. He was moreover accused, rightly or wrongly, of many fantastic peculiarities of doctrine. Whether then it was for offences against discipline that he was condemned, or for offences against sound doctrine, there is nothing to indicate that the doctrine of Restitution entered into the charge. I do not, of course, affirm that it did not enter. But it would be an absurd method of reasoning to say : If Origen was condemned it was probably for the heresy of Restitution, and then to maintain that Restitution is a heresy partly on the ground that it was condemned in the person of Origen at Alexandria. Doubtless there are many who hold Restitution to be a heresy ; but so long as they condescend to reason with us they must not assume as a certainty the very point which, in our controversy, is *adhuc sub judice.*

'The condemnation of Origen, on whatever grounds it was based, was not universal ; he continued to teach, and to meet with the respect due to a great and orthodox teacher and confessor, in Jerusalem, Cæsarea, and Tyre, for about twenty years, till his death in 253. At Alexandria itself his disciples

abounded : Heraclas, successor to Demetrius, Diony-
sius, his successor, Pierius, and many others, followed
in his steps, though I do not presume to say that all
of them accepted all his opinions. It was no expiring
or inconspicuous school of heretics which drew down
the wrath of Methodius. There was no breach of
historical continuity between Origen and his great
follower, S. Gregory Nyssen, who expressly states his
conviction of the ultimate salvation of all men. If for
any time the hope of Restitution had died out, the
revival of it, which we are about to consider, would
have been connected, not with the name of Origen,
but with that of the teacher who revived it. If, then,
we hear little about Restitution during these years, it
can hardly be because it was not mooted : [1] it was
certainly not because Origen's book περὶ ἀρχῶν was
unknown to the Church until it was translated by
Rufinus A.D. 398. In the West no doubt this was the
case ; but not in the East. No doubt the rise of the
Arian troubles tended to put all other controversies
out of sight ; still I can hardly think that the doctrine
would have been left quite unnoticed if it had been
regarded as a very serious error.[2]

'Into the revival of the Origenistic controversy

---

[1] Pusey, *What is of Faith*, p. 125.

[2] It is worth noticing how Rufinus, though he does not apparently
accept Origen's doctrine of Restitution, yet does not treat it as serious
error ; for in the preface to his translation of the περὶ ἀρχῶν he tells us
that he had corrected heretical passages ; but the passages advocating
Restitution are left standing in his version.

I do not intend to enter at any great length. The most vigorous assailant of Origen was one who had formerly been a follower of him, Theophilus of Alexandria. He began the battle by writing, in the year 400, a letter to the synods of Palestine and Cyprus,[1] against Origen and the Origenists, accusing them of self-mutilation, of denying our Lord's Godhead, of expecting the ultimate destruction of the body, of holding various errors about the angels, their fall, and their reception of the Jewish sacrifices, of approving astrology ; but of Restitution he says not a word.

'In his first Paschal letter[2] (A.D. 401) Theophilus accuses Origen of teaching that Christ's kingdom will have an end, and 'the devil will rise again to the height whence he fell,' and that Christ will, one day, suffer to redeem the devils ; as also of forbidding prayer to Christ; but again nothing about Restitution. Nor is it mentioned in the Paschal letters of 402[3] and 404 ; both of which are full of the heresies of Origen. It is hardly conceivable that Theophilus should so often have passed over this conspicuous point in the course of four documents, mainly directed against Origen, which fill about fifty-eight columns in Migne's edition, if he had considered Restitution a dangerous heresy.

'The controversy turned aside, for reasons which I need not detail, from Origen, who was dead, to

---

[1] Translated in S. Jerome, t. i. c. 759 (ed. Migne).
[2] *Ibid.* c. 779.   [3] *Ibid.* c. 792.

S. John Chrysostom, who was living ; and for almost a century and a half (from 404 to 541) Origenism was left alone. In the latter year, however, a violent attack was made upon Origen and his disciples. The theological emperor Justinian addressed to a Home Synod (σύνοδος ἐνδημοῦσα) consisting of those bishops whose sees were near Constantinople, or who frequented the imperial city from motives of interest, a long letter of censure of Origen. It was a letter as tedious as it was violent ; it showed a curious ignorance of Origen's mind ; it was partly based upon forged acts of S. Peter of Alexandria ; it was couched in language which would have befitted a gladiator cursing a panther rather than an emperor dealing with the theologian whom Ambrose copied and Athanasius revered. He closes his tirade with ten anathemas which he desired the Synod to affirm. The ninth of these runs : " If any one says, or thinks, that the punishment of demons and wicked men is for a time and that it will some day have an end, or that there will be a restitution and restoration (*redintegrationem*) of demons and wicked men ; let him be anathema." [1]

' To this letter the Home Synod seems to have replied, not by endorsing the emperor's anathemas as they stood, but by drawing up fifteen anathemas of their own, which cover much the same ground as those of the emperor. But on the question of Restitution there is a singular difference between their language

[1] Baronius, *Ann. Eccl.* an. 538.

and his. In their first anathema they condemn "the mythical pre-existence of souls, and the prodigious restitution which follows upon it ; " that is to say, they condemn, not the doctrine of Restitution in general, but that peculiar form of it which "follows upon" Origen's "mythical pre-existence of souls."[1]

'In the year 553 the Fifth General Council assembled in Constantinople.[2] The patriarch Mennas had given place to Eutychius. Justinian was still on the throne, but (perhaps under the influence of his wife Theodora, in whose mind the excitements of theological controversy had succeeded to those of the theatre and of vice) his zeal had greatly turned away from Origen and the Egyptian school, and was kindled against the Antiochene school and the masters of Nestorius. He begins his address to the bishops by recalling the condemnation of Arius, Macedonius, Apollinarius, Magnus, Nestorius, Eutyches; and desires them in like manner to examine and condemn Theodore of Mopsuestia, Theodoret, and Ibas. Of Origen there is not a word, either among those who have been condemned or among those who are to be

---

[1] These anathemas are appended by Labbe (t. ix. col. 395, ed. Florent, 1763) to the acts of the Fifth General Council ; but it is all but universally allowed that they belong, not to that council, but to a previous Home Synod, presumably that in 541 ; though I venture to suggest (as a mere conjecture) that they belong to another Home Synod after the succession of Eutychius to the Patriarchate, and that the acts of 541 have perished. It is not easy to conceive the courtly bishops of the Home Synod venturing to modify the express anathemas of the Emperor.

[2] Labbe, t. ix. col. 171 *sqq.*

examined. On the other hand, among the Catholic Fathers to whom the Emperor professes adherence is specified S. Gregory Nyssen ; and to this profession the Council itself, in its third session, consents.[1]

'The acts of the Council, which are preserved for the most part only in Latin, are in such detail as to fill more than 220 folio columns. In the course of them the doctrine of Restitution is never alluded to ; the name of Origen occurs twice, amid circumstances of great perplexity.

'In the Fifth Session Theodore Ascidas, himself an Origenist, and the chief mover of the condemnation of Theodore of Mopsuestia, argues, in favour of the lawfulness of condemning dead writers, that "we find many others also anathematised after death, Origen among them ; and if one will go back to the times of Theophilus of holy memory, and further, he will find him anathematised after death ; a course which has even now been taken with respect to the same person by your holiness, and by Vigilius, most religious Pope of old Rome."[2]

'The condemnation by Theophilus has already been discussed. But to what does Theodore refer in the phrase, "even now"? Hefele reasons with some justice that it cannot refer to a condemnation of Origen in some previous session of the General Council of which the acts have been lost ; because, if

---

[1] Labbe, t. ix. col. 200.

[2] 'Quod etiam nunc in ipso fecit et vestra sanctitas et Vigilius.' —Labbe, *ibid.* col. 272, D.

the question of condemning the dead had once been decided by the Council in favour of condemning Origen, no doubt with the consent of the Nestorian party, there could have been no further discussion as to the lawfulness of condemning the dead Nestorianiser, Theodore. But the suggestion of Hefele, that the phrase refers to the condemnation of Origen in the Home Synod of 541 seems hardly possible ; for at that time Eutychius (who is addressed as *Vestra Sanctitas*) was not patriarch, nor indeed did he come to Constantinople before 552, " a few days " before the death of Mennas.[1] The only theory that I can suggest to explain the words of Theodore Ascidas is one which is purely conjectural. We learn, from the Life of Eutychius, that that prelate, on his arrival at Constantinople, won the affection of Justinian by justifying the condemnation of dead heretics by the example of Josiah's dealings with the bones of the priests of Bethel ; and indeed owed his appointment to the patriarchate mainly to this opinion. Is it not likely that, on his accession, Justinian may have proposed to him, either by himself or in a Home Synod, a condemnation of Origen which Vigilius had signed, and which Eutychius then signed ? If this should be allowed, I should venture to suspect that the anathemas which are usually ascribed to the Synod of 541 are really those of Eutychius in 552 or early in 553 ; and that the milder tone of them as compared

---

[1] *Vita S. Eutychii*, iii. 23. (Migne, *P.G.* t. 86. c. 2300 D.)

with Justinian's letter is due, not to the courage of the
bishops of 541 modifying the Emperor's words, but
to the mollifying effect upon the Emperor's mind of
eleven years and the diverted course of controversy.
In this case the acts of 541 have probably perished.
The acts of the hypothetical Home Synod of 552
would stand in the archives of the Church of Constantinople in immediate proximity to those of the
Fifth General Council. In both Councils there
would be the same emperor, the same patriarch,
probably many of the same bishops, the same city,
possibly even the same year. It would not then be
improbable that the acts of the two Councils would
be confused and read together as one ; as has hap-
pened in several other cases. In that way we should
be able to account for the statement of several writers
that the Fifth General Council had examined and
condemned Origen, though of his condemnation there
is hardly a trace in the acts, and of his examination
no trace at all. Of course this suggestion of a Home
Synod in 552 or 553 is purely hypothetical, but it
seems to me not improbable, and it affords a way of
reconciling various facts which I can see no other way
of reconciling.

'However, the matter is of small importance. If
Origen was condemned in the General Council before
the Fifth Session there is no record of the points for
which he was condemned. Even if the General
Council adopted and endorsed the anathemas as-

cribed to the Home Synod of 541, they only condemned a form of Restitution which I do not wish to
uphold. I am almost sorry to have spent so much
space upon a point which has little more than an
antiquarian interest.

'In the acts of the Fifth General Council the name
of Origen occurs once more. The proceedings were
summed up in fourteen anathemas touching upon
various points of the heresies ascribed to Theodore,
Theodoret and Ibas. In the eleventh anathema
we read : " If anyone doth not anathematise
Arius, Eunomius, Macedonius, Apollinarius, Nestorius, Eutyches, Origen, with all their impious writings
and all other heretics who are condemned and anathematised by the Holy Catholic and Apostolic
Church, and the aforesaid four holy Councils ; and
also those persons who were or are imbued with
doctrines like to those of the aforesaid heretics, and
have persisted or do persist unto death in their im-
piety—let him be anathema." [1]

'Now it is obvious that the name of Origen is
suspicious in this place. The sentence is not against
the heretics named, but against those who should
hold with them, as with heretics already condemned ;
but if Origen was condemned at all by any General
Council it was by this present one. The heretics
who were certainly condemned by this Council are
not mentioned in this anathema. All the others who

---

[1] Labbe, t. ix. col. 376.

are named in it had been condemned in previous General Councils, but not so Origen. All the others stand in their true chronological order ; but Origen, who ought to have stood first, is put last. All the others were condemned for heresies respecting the Holy Trinity and the Incarnation ; but the errors usually attributed to Origen concern a different class of subjects—the origin and the destiny of the creature. Most of the others, if not all, had been discussed in the present Council ; but Origen is (as we have seen) only mentioned once, and then obliquely, in the discussions. The general effect of the list of names is as if a modern Synod should condemn " Luther, Calvin, Cranmer, Hoadley, and Eckhart." It is possible that Eckhart was in error ; but at all events he was not a Protestant, and did not live after Hoadley.

'On the whole, then, I am strongly disposed to agree with those who consider the name of Origen in the eleventh anthema an interpolation. It does not necessarily follow from this that Origen was not condemned by the Council. There are several writers quoted by Dr. Pusey who testify that it did condemn him.[1] None of them are evidence of the first class ; there are in some cases repetitions, in others inconsistencies, which impair their testimony. At the most, if the Council condemned Origen, there is no evidence at all that it condemned him for his teaching on Restitution. Indeed, there is one fact which tells

[1] *What is of Faith*, p. 137 ff.

considerably on the other side. A very great part of
the discussions of the Council are concerned with
Theodore of Mopsuestia, in discovering and stating
whose heresies considerable skill was shown by some
of the bishops. But Theodore himself writes : " He
summed up all things in heaven and earth in Christ, as
if making by Him a compendious renovation and com-
pletion (*adintegrationem*) of the whole creature. But
this will be in the world to come, when all men and
also reasonable virtues shall look to Him, as must be,
and shall obtain concord among themselves and their
original peace." [1] In several such passages as this
Theodore declares himself to believe the final destruction of sin ; yet his faith on this point never seems to
have been charged against him in the Council.

' On the whole, then, I think I am justified in
summing up the relation of Councils to the hope of
the extirpation of evil in these sentences. It is very
uncertain whether the Fifth General Council condemned Origen at all ; if it did, it is still more uncertain whether it condemned him for his doctrine of
Restitution ; if it condemned his doctrine of Restitution it does not follow that it condemned all hope of
a final restoration of all men to obedience. It is
certain that local Councils condemned Origen ; it is
quite uncertain whether they condemned him for his
doctrine of Restitution, with the exception of the
Home Synod of 541, which so expressly condemned

---

[1] *In Ephes.* i. 10 (Swete, i. 30).

his peculiar doctrine as to leave the doctrine which we maintain untouched. The only censure which would fall upon our heads is that universal condemnation of Restitution contained in Justinian's anathemas. As we are appealing in these pages to Catholics who have had their eyes open to the evil of Erastianism, I need hardly plead with them that the theological decrees of an Emperor are no more worthy of deference than the ecclesiastical decisions of the Privy Council.

'But I would entreat my readers to consider the significance of this silence of the Church's Councils. The doctrine of Restitution was pressed upon the Church's notice all through the period of the General Councils—pressed upon it in a crude and extreme form (for so I must describe the doctrine of Origen), pressed upon it from many sides and by theologians of eminence ; and yet the Church (whom we believe to be the organ of the Holy Spirit) was restrained from any condemnation of that doctrine. The silence of the Holy Ghost is no less venerable than His speech. We must be as jealous against additions to His teaching as against diminutions from it. It is mere rationalism to say that a doctrine of such moment must have been decided. God, who was pleased to leave for centuries unrevealed His own Tri-unity, His method of Redemption, His merciful designs for the heathen, may not improbably have left His Church without a doctrine *de fide* upon the future of the lost. His method seems to have been not to define every possible doctrine but to lay down certain ruling truths by the help of which the Church and her children should be guided in their further inquiries. Where the Church has been silent it may be our duty to be silent too; it cannot be our duty to erect our own conclusions, however probable, into articles of faith.

'But I shall be reminded that conciliar decrees are not the only guidance to the Church's mind and tradition. The agreement universal, or nearly universal, of Catholic teachers is to be regarded as a strong evidence of Catholic tradition. I do not think this evidence is ever so conclusive as that of a conciliar decree. A council met together under special invocation of the Holy Spirit to inquire carefully into a supposed heresy; lines of tradition converged and balanced each other; and finally the decree of a General Council, accepted by the whole Church, expressed the common sense of the Church and her tradition. Whereas particular writers then, as now, gave expression to the tradition which they had inherited, coloured by their own speculations. The teachings, then, of individual Fathers are not equally conclusive with the decisions of a Council; yet they should be considered with deep respect.

'Let us, then, consider what is the real voice of Catholic tradition, as represented in the Fathers, with regard to the hope which we advocate, that evil will be extirpated and all men will become obedient to God. My conclusion, which I shall hope to establish, is that the Fathers say nothing to forbid us to entertain our hope.

'The concluding 135 pages of Dr. Pusey's treatise consists of a *catena*, compiled with his usual learning, of "testimonies to the belief of everlasting punishment." It will be noticed that a very considerable portion of this *catena* is of no controversial value, because it merely quotes passages which speak of "eternal condemnation." No Christian doubts "eternal condemnation," because our Saviour speaks of it: where the doubt comes in is as to the meaning of "eternal." The repetition of the word does not prove that it means "everlasting." Nevertheless I quite recognise that many of these witnesses do speak of everlasting punishment; but, as I said before, everlasting punishment is not the same thing as everlasting sin. While my hope is strong against the latter, I have little care about the former. There is a touching inscription often to be seen on crosses erected as memorials of missions, in Tyrolese villages: "Nur keine Todsünde." So long as one may hope for the deliverance of ourselves and of all men from sin we can well leave the continuance of punishment in the merciful and just hands of our Redeemer.

'It would be impossible for me to go into detail through all the passages quoted by Dr. Pusey. It will perhaps suffice if I select from his list a few

F

writers, not because they are more favourable to my view than others, for this is not the case, but because they hold deservedly the highest rank among Christian teachers.[1]

'S. Jerome speaks frequently of "eternal punishment," and no doubt understands "eternal" to mean "everlasting." He condemns the opinion that the devil can repent, as encouraging men to sink easily into sins. He says excellently that God "so spares as to judge ; so judges as to be merciful." He mentions among Origen's errors "the restitution of all to an equal state."[2] But he does not (so far as Dr. Pusey's citations go, nor can I supplement them) base his testimony upon tradition, or upon anything but his own interpretation (sometimes allegorical) of Holy Scripture. In a word, he argues for everlasting punishment in precisely the same manner in which Origen argues against it.

'Again, when S. Jerome argues against the notion that "after a long revolution and infinite ages there shall be a restoration of all things, and the glory of all who have been on probation be one "[3]—when he argues that then the common sinner and the mother of our Lord, Gabriel and Satan, will be all one, and all the past as nothing, he is arguing perhaps against Origen, but certainly not against us. We do not con-

---

[1] Pusey, p. 232 ff.   [2] S. Hieron. Ep. 94.
[3] S. Hieron. *in Jonam* iii. 6, 7, quoted in Dr. Pusey, *Sermon on Everlasting Punishment*, p. 29.

ceive that the past will be forgotten; our difficulty rather is, how we who are forgiven can learn to forgive ourselves. We are satisfied with the hope that sinners, like saints, will learn to serve and obey God; and no more expect than we desire to see the persecutor on an equality with the martyr.

'S. Augustine [1] would "hold a peaceable dispute *cum misericordibus nostris* who will not believe that the punishment of the lost will be everlasting (*sempiternam*); " and he attempts to refute them by supposing that they held a constant oscillation of souls between holiness and sin, between felicity and misery. This notion may be a just conclusion from Origen's theory of pre-existence; it certainly is not a necessary result of the hope that all will be " saved and come unto the knowledge of the truth." [2] S. Augustine refutes the notion by saying that Origen has been condemned by the Church,[3] and that the doctrine is absurd, and, as regards the salvation of Satan, *contra recta Dei verba.*

' Without further argument on the general question he goes on to consider some childish notions that Baptism or Communion, the prayers of the saints, or almsdeeds would ensure the sinner against everlasting punishment. Again we notice that what S. Augustine condemns is not what we uphold. What is specially noteworthy is that he treats even Origenists, not as heretics, but as *misericordes nostri.*

[1] *De Civ. Dei*, xxi. 17.   [2] 1 Tim. ii. 4.
[3] This was written about 425, *i.e.* 125 years before the Fifth General Council.

' In the "Enchiridion "[1] he speaks of "some, yea, very many" who based their opinion that punishment would have an end, not on Holy Scripture, but upon their own desire ; and permits them to suppose, if they pleased, that the pains of the damned would, after certain intervals of time, be in some degree mitigated. It might be argued that if sinners go on for ever adding sin to sin their punishment will for ever increase. When the Roman Church[2] tolerates the hope that, in time, the penalty of sense will cease and only the penalty of loss remain, she seems to admit that in time the sinner will cease to sin, and therefore cease to incur fresh pains. This suggestion of S. Augustine, amplified by subsequent writers, seems to me to answer very nearly to our hope. That sinners will cease to sin is our hope : that by their long persistence in sin they have permanently so dulled their eyes that they can receive much less than they might have received of the beatific vision, is the fear that walks hand in hand with the hope. I cannot but think that there is (if I may say so with respect) a Manichean tone about S. Augustine's preceding words : *Post resurrectionem vero facto universo et completo judicio, suos fines habebunt civitates duæ, una scilicet Christi, altera diaboli ; una bonorum, altera malorum.*[3]

' Dr. Pusey says, very truly, that "Origenism was not attractive to the practical Western mind." Nor

[1] Ch. cxii. (tom. vi. col. 404).
[2] See Petavius, quoted by Newman, *Grammar of Assent*, p. 417.
[3] *Enchir.* cxi. (col. 403).

was it more attractive to the rhetorical Eastern mind. The very amplification of the subject, the heaping up of long adjectives, in which such writers as S. Chrysostom indulge, show how ready they were for the most part to use the ready instrument of boundless threats to crush sin, how little disposed to inquire patiently if God was not minded to destroy it by the surer force of His redeeming love. What I would specially call attention to is this, that the Eastern Fathers (as quoted by Dr Pusey) base their threats of endless wrath, not upon tradition, but upon their private inferences from Holy Scripture; that they do not, as far as this matter is concerned, turn aside to brand as heresy the Origenism which flourished among them. When they condemn Origen, it is, as we have seen, mostly for other errors. That S. Gregory of Nyssa acquired and maintained, in spite of his Restitutionism, a high place as a saint and doctor, is a fair indication that his doctrine was not regarded as heretical.

'I do not, then, urge that most of the Fathers believed in Restitution; on the contrary, most of them believed in the endlessness of punishment. The question whether they believed in the perpetuity of sin was not presented to them. It is practically a new problem; but the answer to it must be built upon old foundations. There are two or three positions defined by the Fathers which must be considered if we would arrive at a satisfactory conclusion. The one is the unity of the human race in Christ. Another is S. Augustine's statement : " *Naturæ omnes, quoniam naturarum prorsus omnium Conditor summe bonus est, bonæ sunt* ; " [1] so that in all creatures, however debased, there remains still something that is good. S. Augustine also draws, in reference to a different question, a very clear distinction between *semper esse* and *æternitas*,[2] which might be brought to bear upon the present question. But the consideration of these points would carry me away from the subject to which I have restricted myself. I proposed merely to inquire whether there was either in the decrees of Councils or in the tradition of the Fathers anything to make it impossible for a Catholic to hope that God's victory will be complete, and will be the entire ex- tirpation of sin and the subjugation of every man to His obedience. I think I have shown that no Council which has authority over us has condemned even the Restitutionism of Origen, which involves indeed, but far exceeds, the hope for which I plead. I am con- fident that it might be shown (though in these few pages I cannot show it exhaustively) that the Fathers, as a rule, hardly go beyond the Councils : they mostly believe, no doubt, in the endlessness of punishment, but they base their belief, not on the tradition which has been handed down to them, but on their private interpretations of Holy Scripture, as to which we are

---

[1] *Enchir.* xii. (col. 349).
[2] *De Civ. Dei*, xii. 15 (tom. vii. 505).

at liberty to differ from them.   As to the hope of the destruction of evil they say little or nothing, because the case was not presented to them.

' I venture, then, to maintain our liberty as Catholics to hold the view which is defended in these pages ; though in this, and in all other matters, I desire to submit myself to the authority of the Holy Catholic Church, and to the judgment of men wiser and better than myself.   Both as a guarantee that my opinion is not against the teaching of the Church, and as an assurance that it is consistent with Christian love and awe, I reckon it among my great happinesses that I have your concurrence in the main outlines of what I have written.

' Believe me, ever yours most affectionately,

' HERBERT H. JEAFFRESON.'

PRINTED BY
SPOTTISWOODE AND CO., NEW-STREET SQUARE
LONDON